W9-BZT-293

LIFE DURING THE GREAT CIVILIZATIONS

Ancient Egypt

LIFE DURING THE GREAT CIVILIZATIONS

Ancient Egypt

Jim R. Eddy

BLACKBIRCH PRESS
An imprint of Thomson Gale, a part of The Thomson Corporation

Detroit • New York • San Francisco • San Diego • New Haven, Conn. • Waterville, Maine • London • Munich

For more information, contact
Blackbirch Press
27500 Drake Rd.
Farmington Hills, MI 48331–3535
Or you can visit our Internet site at http://www.gale.com

Photo credits: see page 47.

LIBRARY OF CONGRESS CATALOGING-IN-PUBLICATION DATA

Eddy, Jim R., 1952–
Ancient Egypt / by Jim R. Eddy.
p. cm. — (Life during the great civilizations)
Includes bibliographical references and index.
ISBN 1-4103-0528-7 (hardcover : alk. paper)
1. Egypt—Civilization—To 332 B.C.—Juvenile literature. 2. Egypt—Social life and customs—To 332 B.C.—Juvenile literature. I. Title. II. Series.

DT61.E28 2005
932—dc22 2004020020

Printed in United States
10 9 8 7 6 5 4 3 2 1

Contents

INTRODUCTION

The Enduring Egyptian Society

Life and civilization in ancient Egypt were possible because of the annual flooding of the Nile. This river flows through the largest desert on the planet. Its floods brought huge quantities of freshwater and the deposit of silt, earth, and minerals that had been carried by the water. This natural fertilizer and the water of the Nile made Egypt a great agricultural center. Because the Egyptians did not need to travel to hunt game and gather edible plants, they were able to set up villages and towns along the river's banks. Soon brick makers, carpenters, potters, weavers, and other craftspeople were able to supply the population with items that improved their lives. Even so, farming was so essential to the Egyptians that they called their nation *Kemet*, which means the black land.

The African nation of Kemet was formed in 3100 B.C. when King Menes united two separate kingdoms into one country. He ruled Upper Egypt in the south and conquered the northern kingdom of Lower Egypt. All the people who had settled these lands influenced a culture that had been developing from about 5000 B.C. Africans from Nubia, Syrians and Persians from the Middle East, and others were united into one people under the rule of a king whom they considered to be a god. The king was called a *pharaoh* and was believed to possess magical powers. Among these powers was the ability to bring about the annual flooding of the Nile.

Opposite Page: An ancient Egyptian king celebrates the defeat of an enemy. As pharaoh, the king was believed to be a living god.

Ancient Egyptian farmers relied heavily on the annual flooding of the Nile River.

When the annual flood failed to occur, crops decreased and the people went hungry. Egyptians took this as a sign that the gods were unhappy with the people. Every aspect of life was affected by the desire to keep the gods happy. The Egyptians developed a government and culture based on their religious beliefs. Egyptian religion, culture, and government helped the people build one of the greatest civilizations in the world.

Egyptian civilization developed in the isolated Nile Valley, cut off by deserts, mountains, and the sea. No other culture of the time was so complex and elaborate. Egyptian civilization became the envy of neighboring nations and has fascinated the world in all the centuries that have followed.

CHAPTER ONE

The Egyptian Social Pyramid

Ancient Egyptian society was strictly divided into distinct levels, or classes. Together, the levels resembled a pyramid. At the top was the pharaoh, the king of Egypt. Below the pharaoh and his family were the nobles and priests. They served the pharaoh as assistants in running the kingdom. The middle level included doctors, scribes, soldiers, and artisans, whose work still amazes people around the world. At the base of the social pyramid was the vast majority of Egyptians. These peasants and slaves built temples and pyramids, took care of homes, worked the fields, and tended herds and flocks. Society at large was fanatical in the desire to preserve this way of life. This fanaticism led to a civilization so stable that it lasted five thousand years.

The Pharaoh and the Royal Family

Because a pharaoh was considered to be a living god, only the highest social ranks could approach the king and his family. The middle class and ordinary people were kept away from the pharaoh. A few lucky people might catch a glimpse of the pharaoh during festivals or processions when he went out in public. One such event occurred each year when the pharaoh used his power as a living god to bring about (at least in the beliefs of his people) the annual flooding of the Nile, which caused agriculture to flourish. In the 1300s B.C., one nobleman, Kheruef, wrote an eyewitness account of a celebration held by Pharaoh Amenhotep III:

The glorious appearance of the king at the great double doors in his palace, "The House of Rejoicing"; ushering in the officials, the king's friends, the chamberlain, the men of the gateway, the king's acquaintances, the crew of the barge, the castellans [keepers of a fort or castle], and the king's dignitaries. Rewards were given out in the form of "Gold of Praise," and ducks and fish of gold, and they received ribbons of green linen, each person being made to stand according to his rank. They were fed with food as part of the king's breakfast: bread, beer, oxen, and fowl. They were directed to the lake of His Majesty to row in the king's barge. They grasped the towropes of the Evening Barge and the prow rope of the Morning Barge, and they towed the barges at the great place. They stopped at the steps of the throne.[1]

Ordinary citizens saw the pharaoh only on rare occasions. Amenhotep III (above) once appeared at the doors of his palace during a celebration.

The Nobles and Priests

Nobles like Kheruef were from wealthy landowning families whose social rank was second only to the royal household. Nobles controlled the people who worked their great estates. As rent, the nobles received most of the food that was raised. Sales of the crops increased the nobles' wealth. Nobles often used this money to build their own cities and temples. These privileges made Egypt's nobles a very powerful force.

Power in the kingdom was also held by nomarchs, the governors of Egyptian states called *nomes*. The king chose nobles to fill these offices. Nomarchs held such great power that they even gathered their own armies, which were not always loyal to the king. Some pharaohs were so unwise or weak that their power ebbed away, enabling a nomarch to kill off the royal family and become the new pharaoh. At other times, the whole royal family would die out, and a powerful nomarch would become the pharaoh.

The pharaoh was the leading religious figure of the nation. He was seen as a god and as a mediator between the other Egyptian gods. A pharaoh was required to carry out daily rituals in each temple, but since he could not possibly visit all of Egypt's temples each day, a high priest was appointed to carry out these duties. Temple priests oversaw the religion of Egypt. Because over the centuries they had received gifts of land from pharaohs and nobles, priests were also an important landowning group. Some temples owned so much land that the priests were incredibly wealthy. They used this wealth to maintain and enlarge the temples. The amazing objects that filled the temples, palaces, and tombs were created by Egypt's specialized workers.

A high priest at each temple carried out the pharaoh's religious duties. Pictured is the Temple of Luxor, containing a mosque built thousands of years later.

The Artisans and Professionals

Egyptian art has fascinated the world for many centuries. These artifacts were created by artisans, people with specialized skills, who occupied the middle layer of the Egyptian social pyramid. Artisans included carpenters, stone carvers, goldsmiths, potters, and weavers. They manufactured benches, chests, jewelry, cooking pots, perfume bottles, clothing, and all the other goods that Egyptians needed.

Egyptian artisans painted detailed designs on this casket made to hold the body of a pharaoh.

Laborers and artisans use their skills to build a temple.

Scribes and doctors were Egypt's professionals. Scribes were taught to read and write and to keep all of Egypt's records. The pharaohs used scribes to write letters to foreign kings and to tally the taxes that were collected throughout Egypt. By performing these duties, some scribes became so important that they were able to move up the social scale to the level of the nobles and priests.

Professional soldiers held the same social position as artisans. Their fighting skills enabled a pharaoh to conquer neighboring kingdoms. Soldiers had more opportunity to advance in their social station than any other group in ancient Egypt. Successful fighting men were promoted to become officers, sometimes even generals. At the right time, a powerful general might be able to seize the throne and declare himself the pharaoh of Egypt.

From Servant to Egyptian General

During the 2300s b.c., a man named Weni was so successful as a servant to Pharaoh Pepi I that he was promoted to the office of general. As described in A. Gardiner's book *Egypt of the Pharoahs*, wall carvings on Weni's tomb tell how his life had changed:

> When His Majesty inflicted punishment upon the Asiatics and Sand–dwellers, His Majesty made an army of many tens of thousands from the entire [land of] Upper Egypt. . . .It was I who was in command of them, though my office was [merely] that of an Overseer of the tenants of the Palace, because I was well suited to prevent one from quarrelling with his fellow, to prevent one of them from taking bread or sandals from a wayfarer, to prevent any one of them from taking a loin–cloth from any village, to prevent any one of them from taking any goat from any [person]. . . . This army returned in peace, it had slain troops in its many tens of thousands.

The People

Ordinary people made up the next lowest social class in ancient Egypt. They performed hard labor so that the upper classes could devote their time to running their estates and serving the pharaoh. Most Egyptians were peasants who farmed the land. They harvested wheat, onions, garlic, and other crops for Egypt's people. They also raised goats, cattle, ducks, and geese.

When a pharaoh wanted to rebuild a city, enlarge a temple, or construct a fort, the work was carried out by ordinary people. Most of this work was completed during the months when the Nile flooded and slowly subsided, leaving behind rich soil for the year's crops. One project in early Egypt was building pyramids for the pharaohs and their families, nobles, and priests. People were paid for this exhausting labor. They were thus able to earn a living while waiting for the floodwaters to recede so they could return to their fields and flocks.

Slaves

At the bottom of the social pyramid were slaves. Often, slaves were those who had sold themselves as workers in order to pay off their debts. Other slaves were foreigners captured in war. Most slaves worked in the households of the pharaohs and the nobles. Some tended gardens built around the great houses of the kingdom. Others did all the cooking and baking, or worked as nurses to raise the children of the pharaohs and the nobles. Slaves actually carried out the management of their owners' estates, seeing that crops were planted, cared for, and harvested successfully. Some slaves even learned the skills of artisans. Many became scribes in service to the pharaohs, the nobles, and the priests of the temples.

Some people sold themselves into slavery to clear their debts. At right is a bronze figurine of a bound slave.

It was not impossible for a slave to rise above his or her social station. Many were freed by their owners, and some even married members of their owners' families. However, even after they rose to higher social ranks, these people were generally looked down upon for having once been slaves. It might take generations for a freed slave's descendants to be fully accepted into Egyptian society.

CHAPTER TWO

Daily Life

Like the Egyptian society as a whole, ancient Egyptian families featured distinct levels. All fathers were the heads of families. They were responsible for making all the decisions that affected their families' lives. Fathers determined which chores family members and servants would do. When to enlarge a home or to make a purchase, what religious duties to carry out and when, and any other decision that affected the family as a whole was made by the father.

Women and Children

Egyptian women were ruled by their fathers until they married. Afterward, they were ruled by their husbands. Still, Egyptian women had more rights than women in other nations. A nobleman's wife or daughter could inherit and run his estates. A woman could choose whom to marry, ask for a divorce, begin lawsuits, travel on her own, and choose what kind of clothing to wear. In a divorce, a woman kept a third of her family's property. A widow also received a third of the property when her husband died, while her children received the other two-thirds. About 1791 B.C. a man named Uah wrote a will that not only leaves property to his wife, but shows his love for her.

Opposite Page: An Egyptian father relaxes with his wife and children in this wall painting.

> I am making a title to property to my wife, the woman of Ges–ab, Sat–Sepdu's daughter Sheftu, who is called Teta, of all things given to me by my brother, the devoted servant of the superintendent of works, Ankh–ren, as to each article in its place of everything that he gave me. She shall give it to any she desires of her children that she (has borne) me. I am giving to her the eastern slaves, 4 persons, that my brother ... gave to me. She shall give them to whomsoever she will of her children. As to my tomb, let me be buried in it with my wife, without allowing anyone to move ... to it. Moreover, as to the apartments that my brother ... built for me, my wife (shall dwell) therein, without allowing her to be put (forth) thence on the ground by any person.[2]

Certain jobs were open to Egypt's women. Some could work as artisans, and a few even became scribes. Women were hired as dancers and musicians. They also held important positions in the nation's temples. A high priestess had the job of awakening Amon–Ra, the sun god, each day so that he could row the sun in a boat across the sky. Most women, however, were wives and mothers and were responsible for running households and raising children. Mothers saw to their children's needs, made their clothing, and taught them basic skills.

Egyptian women could work at certain jobs, but most looked after their families at home.

Young children were usually free to amuse themselves. They played games and explored their villages and the banks of the Nile. To indicate their status, children wore sidelocks, a single lock of hair that was allowed to grow from the side of the head. At adolescence,

Hatshepsut, the Female King

In the 1400s B.C. Pharaoh Thutmose I had a daughter who became a great ruler of Egypt. As was the royal custom, Princess Hatshepsut married her half–brother who became Pharaoh Thutmose II. He lived for only a short time and chose his nephew to become Pharaoh Thutmose III. Since this boy was so young, Hatshepsut was chosen to rule the kingdom until he became an adult. Thutmose III grew into a man more interested in war and conquest than in ruling the kingdom, so Hatshepsut continued her reign. Since pharaohs were always men, she began wearing the costume, a fake beard, and the crown of a male ruler.

Hatshepsut encouraged trade, especially with neighboring kingdoms in Africa, and became one of Egypt's great builders. Her beautiful temple at Deir el–Bahri is one of the most magnificent ever built by the ancient Egyptians. After her death, Thutmose III took over all the duties of a pharaoh. At some point most of the references to Hatshepsut as pharaoh were destroyed, perhaps to maintain the idea that all pharaohs were men.

this sidelock was shaved, and the carefree days of childhood were over. Adolescents began the important task of preparing to be adults.

Children were allowed to hold only the same jobs as their parents, so choosing a career was impossible. Daughters were taught to be good housekeepers, wives, and mothers. Sons studied their fathers' trades. Sons of farmers became farmers, those of artisans became artisans, and noblemen's sons were trained to run their families' estates. When children married, they set up their own homes in the same village or city where they grew up.

Homes

All homes, even the pharaoh's palaces, were made of sun-dried brick. These structures had few windows, to keep out as much of the harsh

A modern-day Egyptian woman and her daughter make bread. Daughters in ancient Egypt learned household skills from their mothers.

desert sunlight as possible. Most homes were small and were used for eating and sleeping. Most daily life occurred under canopies set up on the flat rooftops at people's homes or in shaded courtyards out of doors so that the Egyptians could take advantage of winds and breezes. This also gave the people a chance to relax and visit with their neighbors. Visiting was the mainstay of social life in ancient Egypt.

Meals were also a social activity for Egyptians. Cooking was often carried out on fires and in ovens shared by several families in a neighborhood. All food was collected as a tax since the ordinary people farmed land owned by the pharaoh. Priests and nobles stored these foods and reserved part for the pharaoh. Each of the priests and nobles also took a share of the food. The remainder was handed out by the priests and nobles to the people. The people would gather at a nearby temple or noble's estate to obtain what they needed each day.

A day's ration of food might include onions, beans, figs, dates, leeks, lettuce, grapes, and wheat flour for bread. Grapes were processed into wine, while grain and honey were used to make beer. Unclean conditions caused most water to be unsanitary. Alcohol in wine and beer made these liquids safe to drink.

Leisure

Food was an important part of the leisure time that Egyptians enjoyed. All festivals involved great feasts celebrated by families, friends, and neighbors. Festivals were the major social events of the year. Great processions were made up and down the Nile in honor of the god who was being celebrated or honored by each festival. Musicians and singers filled the boats to entertain people along the river's banks.

Egyptians also rested on the first day of each week. At these times, the people entertained themselves with picnics, games, dances, wrestling, stick fighting, and hunting. Most hunting was carried out through the use of spears, bows, and arrows. However, the use of the boomerang was borrowed from the people living in central Africa, particularly the nation of Nubia. Dogs were used to track and corner gazelles, water birds, oxen, crocodiles, turtles, hippopotamuses, elephants, and giraffes.

Besides hunting, the people also enjoyed fishing. Eels, catfish, carp, and other kinds of fish filled the Nile and the nation's lakes and streams. Egyptians used many kinds of nets to catch this important source of food. They also used lines and hooks, which were usually made of bronze or copper. Since meat was rarely eaten by ordinary people, fish were an important source of protein in their diets. Even so, few Egyptians ventured to fish in the Mediterranean or Red seas. They viewed oceans as dangerous places at the end of the world.

Hunting was a favorite sport among Egyptians. Below, hunters startle a flock of birds.

Travel

Although they avoided seas and oceans, Egyptians were great travelers. Roads and footpaths lined the banks of the Nile. These were usually used for short trips from town to town. However, the Nile was the main source of transport and the river flowed for hundreds of miles through the kingdom. Cities, temples, and palaces could be visited at spots all along the river. The pharaoh, the royal family, and nobles were the classes who could afford that sort of travel. Each long trip required a great deal of planning and work to carry out. When the pharaoh traveled, hundreds of people were needed to carry out these elaborate expeditions. They not only sailed and rowed the boats, they cooked the food, guarded the travelers, and carried all the goods that the people needed.

Only the wealthy could afford to travel long distances by boat. Ordinary people made short trips on foot.

CHAPTER THREE

Egypt's Gods Promise Eternal Life

According to the Egyptian religion, chaos was the state of the waters that existed at the beginning of time. A mound grew up out of these waters and became the world. A temple crowned the mound of earth and honored the gods who had brought order to the world. Chaos was seen as a force that constantly threatened to flood the earth. The basis of ancient Egypt's religion was pleasing the gods so that chaos and order were kept in balance.

Temple Duties and Responsibilities

Religious duties and responsibilities were at the heart of Egyptian life and civilization. Each community and region in Egypt had its own god or set of gods. When the country was united under the pharaohs, some gods were absorbed into the national religion supported by all the people. All the largest temples and festivals were dedicated to the national gods. However, each temple was built to honor one god.

The temples were built under the direction of the priests, who also arranged and controlled the festivals. All this work was done at great cost. To pay for it, the priests sold some of the sacrifices people made of food, clothing, and other items. They also sold some of the crops that were their share of the nation's taxes. This wealth was used not only to maintain the temple complexes, but also to pay the priests' salaries.

Opposite Page: The Egyptian sky goddess curves her body to cover the earth god.

Some of the sacrifices and taxes that were not sold were used in the daily rituals carried out in the nation's temples. Food was prepared every morning for the god who was believed to live in each temple. These were the same foods eaten by all Egyptians (onions, leeks, figs, dates, wine, and beer). However, meat from oxen, birds, and wild game was served only to the higher classes of society. It was therefore a suitable sacrifice to the gods. The gods ate only the spirit of the food. In the evening, the meal was gathered and served to the priests and servants of the temple.

Priests, priestesses, and the pharaoh were the only people worthy to be servants of the gods. Each morning, the high priest and his most trusted assistant would open the door of the darkened room where the statue of the temple's god was kept. The high priest would enter the room and stand before the statue. The associate priest would hand him a bowl of water and clothing so that the high priest could bathe the statue and dress it in clean clothing. Then the high priest would back out of the room, sweeping away the footprints he

A high priestess makes an offering to a goddess in a temple.

had made in the dust. He closed and sealed the door behind him.

Each temple statue could be seen by all Egyptians only once each year. An annual festival was held in honor of each national god of the kingdom. The statue was removed from its darkened room, carried outside on a litter, and placed aboard a boat. The boat would carry the statue in a great procession of boats that contained the pharaoh, his family and court, and important officials. Ordinary people lined the banks to glimpse the god and their pharaoh.

Bes, a favorite domestic god pictured in this stone relief, watched over a couple's marriage as well as the household.

Household Gods

This religious devotion extended into family life as well. Family gods were those who were worshipped inside the home and as part of the community. Small statues of the god were kept in an altar or shrine that often consisted of a small opening in a wall of the home. Family members filled bowls with food and drink that were placed as sacrifices to the favored god. Prayers were delivered to the god as the sacrifices were presented.

Two of the most popular household gods were Taweret and Bes. Egyptians believed that Taweret, the goddess of birth and the raising of children, could ensure that parents were able to have children and that mothers would be safe during the births of their babies. This goddess was represented as a statue of a pregnant hippopotamus. Bes was the god who was believed to protect the home from all danger as well as the marriage between husband and wife. Statues of this god have been found in the ruins of almost all ancient Egyptian homes.

The mummified body, or akh, served as a home for the soul, or ka. Family members placed items necessary for the afterlife with the akh.

Eternal Life

One of the most important gods was Osiris, the god of the dead. Egyptians believed that he determined if a soul, known as the *ka*, would exist after death or if it would be destroyed. The belief that the body needed to be preserved as the akh, or home for the ka, led to the process of mummification.

The earliest mummies were those of bodies that were simply buried in the desert sand. The heat and dryness of the sand absorbed all the moisture from the corpse, which could last for thousands of years. This process was held to be too simple, however, for important officials, the royal family, and the pharaoh. Mummification became an elaborate and expensive method of preserving bodies. The internal organs were removed and placed in special jars. The openings were filled with salts and special minerals that helped dry out the body. Then the body was wrapped in lengths of linen so that it would retain its shape. Religious symbols, gems, and other special items were woven into the bandages.

A tomb became the home of the akh and the place where the ka would carry out its eternal life. Simple burials contained only a few essential goods, but tombs of nobles and royals became elaborately decorated and furnished burial chambers. Everything the ka would need in the afterlife was placed inside the tomb—food, clothing, furniture, mirrors, games, and other goods.

A temple was also built near the tomb or grave. Family members would come to the temple to offer sacrifices for the ka and to leave food and other essential things the dead might need. Because each Egyptian longed for an easy life after death, they spent their entire lifetimes preparing for their burials.

CHAPTER FOUR

Simple Tools and Magnificent Creations

Egyptians used simple tools to plow the land, irrigate and harvest crops, and build homes and temples. The people used wood, stone, and metal to make their tools. Egyptians used the same simple tools to create some of the most beautiful artifacts ever to exist in the world.

Farming

Hoes and axes made of wood with stone heads helped farmers break up the dry earth. Cattle or the farmers themselves pulled small plows to form the rows where seeds were thrown. Then farmers let their cattle loose to walk over the fields and push the seeds into the ground. Flint was formed into sharp sickle blades used to cut down crops like wheat and barley. Farmers made wooden rakes to gather the harvested stalks into piles. Cattle were driven across the piles to loosen the grain from the stalks. Rakes were used to toss the grain into the air. Breezes blew away the chaff, or remains of the stalks, and the grain fell down into piles that were gathered and ground into flour.

Crops of flax stalks were pounded with stones until the fibers broke down. Women used simple wooden spinners to wind the flax into thread, which was then woven into the fine white linen cloth used for clothing. White cloth kept Egyptians cooler than colored cloth, so it was the most favored in ancient Egypt. Anyone seen wearing clothing of colored cloth was assumed to be a foreign visitor.

Farmers used simple plows drawn by cattle to sow their crops.

Simple stone pickaxes and shovels helped farmers irrigate their fields. A huge system of canals and dikes was built to store and direct water from the floods caused by the Nile. At first, clay pots were used to dip water from canals and artificial lakes so it could be poured onto fields. Later, the center of a long pole was attached to a base so the pole could be moved like a seesaw. A basket was hung from one end of the pole, and a farmer would work the other end. This invention allowed one person to move a great amount of water in a short time.

Structures

Besides being used for farming, water was also an important ingredient for the materials used to build homes. Farmers' homes as well as the palaces of the king were made of simple sun-dried brick. Water, soil, and straw were mixed together and pushed into wooden boxes that

A modern-day farmer moves water from a canal in much the same way as her ancient Egyptian ancestors.

had no tops or bottoms. The mud shapes were left to dry in the sun. More mud was used to fasten the bricks into walls. Brick was used to form roofs where Egyptians could take advantage of breezes while relaxing or sleeping.

Even though Egyptians were master stonemasons and carvers, stone was reserved for the most special Egyptian buildings. Stone temples were set up to honor the gods. Giant obelisks stood outside temples and were carved with messages about individual pharaohs' great deeds. One temple was so huge that two giant statues were built as frames to hold immense doors.

Stone for temples, pyramids, and tombs was quarried from the sides of mountains and from the bedrock beneath the soil. Simple stone and metal chisels were pounded with hammers to form grooves in the face of the selected rock. Wooden spikes were pounded into the grooves and were then soaked with water. The water made the spikes swell so that the grooves were pushed apart, causing the stone to break away in the desired shape. This method was used to quarry all the stone blocks Egyptians used in their building projects. Pharaoh Ahmose I recorded the act of opening a new quarry during his reign:

The carved characters on this obelisk tell of a pharaoh's achievements.

> Year 22 under his majesty, the king of Upper and Lower Egypt, son of the sun, Ahmose, endowed with life. Newly opened were quarries. Beautiful white limestone was extracted for his houses of millions of years (refers to Pharaoh's tomb). ... The stone was dragged by cattle which Asiatics brought from the land of the Phoenicians. Made under the supervision of the ... vigilant superintendent of the lord of the two lands (supervising) the creation of memorials for eternity [in very] great [numbers].[4]

After stone was quarried, sleds and muscle power moved the blocks to the banks of the Nile. They were placed on board boats and ships for transport. Once the blocks arrived at the appointed destination, they were removed and then pulled by sled to the building site.

The Greatest Egyptian Canal

Canals were not only important parts of the Egyptian irrigation system. They were also vital transportation routes. Canals fed by the Nile allowed Egyptian ships and boats to bypass areas of rapids and rocks in the river. Ships were sent through canals to trade with other countries or to carry soldiers who fought to help the pharaoh conquer more land.

One canal was so important that it helped make Egypt one of the world's richest and most powerful nations. In the 1800s, France succeeded in rebuilding this artificial channel that is now called the Suez Canal. Like the early Egyptian canal, it links the Nile with the Red Sea. Many times over the centuries the early canal filled with sand and rocks and had to be redug. By the 600s B.C. Pharaoh Necho ordered his people to reopen the canal. The Greek historian Herodotus wrote about this tremendous undertaking:

> The length of this is a voyage of four days, and in breadth it was so dug that two triremes [boat propelled by three banks of oars] could go side by side driven by oars. In the reign of Necos (Necho) there perished (died) while digging it twelve myriads of the Egyptians (120,000).

The manner in which the Egyptians raised the blocks to tremendous heights is not known. It was such an everyday procedure that the ancient people never recorded how it was done.

Artifacts

Once a pyramid, tomb, or temple was complete, the work of Egypt's finest artisans decorated and filled these magnificent structures. All these goods were made for use by the gods and by the dead in their afterlives. Carpenters built chests for storage, beds, boats, chairs,

The walls of a tomb described the life of the dead person with pictures and writing.

The first Egyptian pyramid was designed to hold the tomb of Pharaoh Djoser (below).

shovels, chariots, and plows. Weavers turned flax into the linen cloth worn by all Egyptians. Potters created pots, jugs, and bowls. Often, they made the simple clay figures of gods that were worshipped in the homes of ordinary people.

The nobles, priests, and the pharaoh hired sculptors to create stone images of themselves as well as statues of the gods. Goldsmiths and painters decorated the items used by the highest classes in ancient Egypt. They also decorated the walls of the stone temples and tombs. A tomb's walls were carved and painted with scenes of the dead person's life on earth as well as scenes of what the person expected in the afterlife. Most Egyptians expected an afterlife of family gatherings, hunting, fishing, festivals, and other forms of entertainment and relaxation.

Architecture and Astronomy

Tombs for the dead as well as temples for the gods were designed by architects who oversaw the armies of masons, sculptors, painters, and laborers who built these creations. Imhotep designed the first Egyptian pyramid as a tomb for Pharaoh Djoser. Early tombs were built in the shape of the flattop tents with sloping sides that had been homes for the early nomadic Egyptians. Imhotep designed a series of these shapes that stacked upon each other. Then the structure was covered with shaped and

smoothed stone. This famous step pyramid still stands in the deserts of Egypt. Later architects filled in the steps to create true pyramids for their employers.

Ramses II's temple at Abu Simbel is aligned to allow the first summer sunlight into its chamber.

All this amazing work was carried out with sophisticated tools made from very basic materials. Ropes and sticks were used like modern tape measures and rulers. It is possible that wheels were used to mark the distances between points that would be the bases of huge structures. Wood, ropes, and stones were used to form tools that showed if a structure was level and straight. Egyptian architects were so skilled that even huge tombs and temples have walls that are only a few inches out of line.

Aligning tomb and temple walls with the stars was important to the ancient Egyptians. The constellations were symbols of Egyptian gods. By using simple tools and technology, tombs were built to face important star groups. Ramses II's great temple at Abu Simbel is so perfectly aligned that the first shaft of summer sunlight shines through the door and lights a statue of the pharaoh on the back wall. The spectacular ability of Egyptians to create such marvels with the simplest of tools allowed them to develop a civilization that will continue to fascinate the world for centuries to come.

Notes

Chapter 1: The Egyptian Social Pyramid

1. Quoted in Barry J. Kemp, *Ancient Egypt: Anatomy of a Civilization*. New York: Routledge, 1993, pp. 215–216

Chapter 2: Daily Life

2. Quoted in Griffith, *Hieratic Papyri from Kahun and Gurob.* London: Bernard Quaritch, 1898

Chapter 3: Egypt's Gods Promise Eternal Life

3. Quoted in RomanceEverAfter, "Tomb Inscription, Ancient Egypt." www.romanceeverafter.com/the_unknown_poets.htm.

Chapter 4: Simple Tools and Magnificent Creations

4. Quoted in Kurt Sethe, *Urkunden der 18. Dynastie*, vol. 1. Leipzig: J.C. Hinrich, 1914, p. 13f.

Glossary

artifact: An item that remains after a civilization ends or disappears.

artisan: A person trained in special skills that allow the person to create objects of art.

chaos: A time of complete disorder and confusion.

flax: A reedlike water plant used to make linen cloth.

flint: An extremely hard stone that can be sharpened to a fine edge.

litter: A long bed with handles that is used to carry a person from place to place; a stretcher.

nomadic: Being on the move from place to place during life.

nomarch: An ancient Egyptian governor of a state or province.

obelisk: A tall, thin stone structure with four sides that slope toward a small pyramid placed on its peak.

sickle: A cutting tool with a long curved blade attached to a long handle; used to cut down crops and grasses.

For More Information

Books

James Cross Giblin, *The Riddle of the Rosetta Stone*. New York: HarperCollins, 1993.

Nathaniel Harris, *Everyday Life in Ancient Egypt*. New York: Franklin Watts, 1994.

George Hart, *Ancient Egypt*. New York: Alfred A. Knopf, 1990.

Jacqueline Morley and Mark Bergin, *An Egyptian Pyramid*. New York: Peter Bedrick, 2001.

Lila Perl Yerkow, *Mummies, Tombs, and Treasure*. Boston: Clarion, 1990.

Web Sites

Aldokkan: Ancient Egyptian Proverbs (www.aldokkan.com/art/proverbs.htm). A list of proverbs and sayings that reflect ancient Egyptian ideas about life, duty, and religious beliefs.

Kibbutz Reshafim: Ancient Egyptian Texts (www.reshafim.org.il/ad/egypt/texts). This site is an excellent source of ancient Egyptian texts. It includes thorough descriptions of how the texts explain Egyptian life and customs. It also includes an extensive list of links to sites concerning the ancient Egyptians.

Life in Ancient Egypt, Carnegie Museum (www.carnegiemnh.org). An excellent collection of articles on ancient Egypt, its people, and society.

Index

Picture Credits

Cover, page 7 © The Art Archive/Egyptian Museum Cairo/Dagli Orti; page 8 © Staffan Widstrand/CORBIS; pages 10, 20 © The Art Archive/Musee de Louvre Paris/Dagli Orti; pages 11, 18, 29 © The Art Archive/Dagli Orti; page 12 © Roger Wood/CORBIS; page 13 © The Art Archive/Bibliotheque des Arts Decoratifs Paris/Dagli Orti; page 16 © Francis B. Mayer/CORBIS; pages 22, 25, 41 © Property of Blackbirch Press; pages 24, 28, 30, 32, 36, 37, 39 Corel Corporation; page 27 © The Art Archive/Ragab Papyrus Institute Cairo/Dagli Orti; page 35 North Wind Picture Archives; page 40 © Archivo Iconografico, S.A./CORBIS

About the Author

Jim R. Eddy has written and edited numerous educational works in association with his business partners, John B. Allen and Clanci Brown Miller. These three friends live and work in Oklahoma City.